SURVIVAL TIPS
FOR
NEW TEACHERS

from
People Who Have Been There
and
Lived to Tell About It

edited by Cheryl Miller Thurston

Cottonwood Press, Inc.

Requests for permission should be addressed to:
    Cottonwood Press, Inc.
    107 Cameron Drive
    Fort Collins, Colorado 80525
    800-864-4297

ISBN 1-877673-27-7

Printed in the United States of America

ACKNOWLEDGMENTS

Cottonwood Press would like to thank the following teachers who have "been there" for their suggestions, tips and advice for new teachers:

Mary Borg; Greeley, Colorado

Rebecca L. Brown; Williston, North Dakota

Sandra J. Burdette; Charleston, West Virginia

Pamela S. Cottrill; Morgantown, West Virginia

Esther Davison; Pine Bluffs, Wyoming

Linda DeVille; Rescue, California

Karyl DiPrince; La Junta, Colorado

Charles A. Eberhard; Pine Bluffs, Wyoming

Janice Ellens; Kalamazoo, Michigan

Amy Enzi; Gillette, Wyoming

Scott C. Ferguson; Virginia Beach, Virginia

Laurell Fogg; Carpenter, Wyoming

Kristen Frohnhoefer; Ellicott City, Maryland

Vicki Gage; Shepherdsville, Kentucky

Janice M. Gifford; Mt. Olivet, Kentucky

Catherine Gilbert; Baltimore, Maryland

Judith A. Granese; Las Vegas, Nevada

Debbie Hartwig; Woodside, California

Mary Harutun; Carbondale, Colorado

Gail Skroback Hennessey; Harpursville, New York

Carolyn Huisjen; Fort Collins, Colorado

Vicki Hurt; Abilene, Texas

Kevin T. Irvine; Fort Collins, Colorado

Pat Jacobson; Cody, Wyoming

Carole Koester; West Palm Beach, California

Randy Larson; Burns, Wyoming

Lynn Lucke Lutkin; Fort Collins, Colorado

Joanna M. Martin; St. Charles, Illinois

Polly Miller; La Junta, Colorado

Jeanne Montembeau; Biddeford, Michigan

Paula Muri; Altoona, Pennsylvania

Shelby Myers-Verhage; Cedar Rapids, Iowa

R.J. Penhallegon; Baltimore, Maryland

Jan Reeder; St. Joseph, Missouri

Saundra Hayn Schaulis; Sunnyvale, California

Heather Smith; Bartlesville, Oklahoma

Ann Spence; Waterford, Pennsylvania

Arla Squires; Fort Collins, Colorado

Jeff Squires; Fort Collins, Colorado

Cheryl Miller Thurston; Fort Collins, Colorado

Dena Tompsett-Hartmann; Fort Collins, Colorado

Leslie Walker; Raton, New Mexico

Rita Wills; Las Vegas, Nevada

TABLE OF CONTENTS

INTRODUCTION

TO NEW TEACHERS . . .

Back in 1972, I began my first teaching job as a mini-skirted 22-year-old who got into trouble the first day for not having a hall pass. I credit my survival the first couple of years to two young female teachers I admired. "What do you do when a kid says he won't do something?" I would ask Linda. She would give me not only suggestions for what to do but also for the words to use as I did it. Somehow having the words ready ahead of time helped me more than anything. Her advice — and her words — always worked for me.

"Don't walk toward an angry, violent kid," another teacher, Mary, told me one day. "Calmly say what you expect him to do, as if you mean it, and walk away, as if it has never even occurred to you that he wouldn't do what you say. You give him a chance to save face." She was right. I mentally thanked her again and again over the years for that piece of intelligent advice.

Succeeding as a teacher involves a combination of courage, luck, skill, knowledge, sensitivity and persistence. If you are a new teacher, listen to teachers with years of experience. They have learned a few things over the years. Not everything will work for you, but it's smart to pay attention and be open to their advice and help.

We all make mistakes on the job and learn from them, but the mistakes of a new teacher are often particularly difficult. They involve a big audience (the students) and consequences that are difficult or even impossible to correct.

For example, a teacher who makes the mistake of not being consistent enough in classroom management makes that mistake in front of 30 or so young people who are quite aware that he has blown it. That's hard to correct, except by starting over, and it's hard to start over in the middle of the year.

On the other hand, a new teacher's inexperience can often be one of her greatest assets. She looks at everything with new eyes. Because she doesn't know that something "just won't work with these kids," she may go ahead and do it, with great success. She often has an excitement about her new job that is infectious, and she may bring life to a classroom as she experiments and feels her way.

Welcome to the world of teaching. Take a look at the advice in this book, collected from experienced teachers all over the country. I hope that some of these words of wisdom will make your new teaching career just a little bit easier and more successful.

Happy teaching!

Cheryl Miller Thurston

To Experienced Teachers . . .

If you have advice that you think should be included in this book, please send it to Cottonwood Press. We are collecting new material to add and would love to have your ideas. We will give you credit for your submission at the front of the next edition.

Please send your ideas to:

Cottonwood Press, Inc.
Attn: Survival Tips for New Teachers Editor
107 Cameron Drive
Fort Collins, CO 80525

Planning
and
Organizing

PLANNING
AND
ORGANIZING

Teachers are some of the most organized people in the world. They *have* to be. If they don't develop a system of planning and organizing that works for them, they flounder, struggle and ultimately sink under the heavy demands.

As a new teacher, you may find that it helps to understand *why* it seems impossible to keep up with everything. Take a look at the facts:

- A typical secondary teacher supervises 150–180 people per day. (Think of a person in the business world who has that much responsibility. He or she would probably be a top-level manager.) Elementary teachers may supervise fewer individuals, but they are responsible for a wider range of subjects.

- Although a teacher manages huge numbers of people, he or she does it without the benefit of a secretary to do any of the paperwork. A typical manager would have at least one secretary to answer phones, type, photocopy, file, staple, etc. Teachers do not.

- In the business world, people can use time at work to prepare for presentations and meetings. Teachers have very little time to actually plan lessons while at school, and most of them have five or more presentations *every single day*.

- The paper work is overwhelming. An average junior high teacher, with six classes a day of 30 students each, has 180 students. If each of them turns in only three papers or tests per week, that's 540 papers per week to grade and record — a whopping 19,440 papers per year! No wonder they have difficulty keeping up.

Learning to plan and organize efficiently is an important job for new teachers. Don't be afraid to experiment. Listen to advice and pointers from veteran teachers, but adapt their methods to fit *your* style. No two teachers work in exactly the same way. Experiment to see what works best for you.

The tips that follow may help you in learning to plan and organize efficiently.

Expect things to take MORE time than
you think they will. A simple little assignment that you
think will take 15 minutes may end up taking the whole
class period.

Expect things to take a lot LESS time
than you think they will. You will sometimes find that
what you had planned for two days will take 15 minutes.
Then you will be facing 30 students with nothing to do
— not a good situation. Always plan more than you think
you could possibly need.

*Planning and
Organizing*

Don't be distraught if you have to trash one day's lesson plan because of an unexpected schedule change. That
change will seem irrelevant by the time May rolls around.

As much as possible, **handle paper only once**.
Fill out forms from the office as you receive them. Decide
immediately what to keep and what to throw out.

You don't have to do things the way the teacher next
door does them. **If *piles* work better than *files*
for you, stick to piles.**

Take a personal time management course. Unless you
are already a genius at time management, it should help.

Keep good notes. Administrators, guidance counselors, parents, etc., constantly turn to teachers for support, help and information about students. An index card on each student, kept in a simple file box in a private place, works well. Be specific, noting dates, incidents, people involved, etc.

> Be prepared to use a lot of out-of-school time for preparation and grading and worrying. You will probably be shocked and horrified by how much time you will need.

Unless you happen to have a copy machine right beside your desk, invest in carbon paper for note writing. Then you'll always have a copy of each note you write to parents, students, other teachers and administrators.

Record daily assignments on a clipboard or chart for students to check after they have been absent. You might also assign each student a "buddy" — a fellow classmate to check with about assignments.

Put homework and extra copies of handouts in special boxes. Students who have been absent can pick up what they need when they return.

Don't be afraid, once in a great while, to "forget" to grade a stack of assignments. If you are totally buried in paper work, it may help you catch up. The world will not end as a result. In fact, the students probably won't even notice.

Planning and Organizing

If you tell a student to correct or redo something, make a note of it. If you forget about it, students will quickly learn they can get away with not doing their assignments. Keep a daily "owed" list with the names of students and what they need to do.

Don't think that you are losing your mind if it feels like you can never catch up. You probably can't.

BUILDING RAPPORT WITH STUDENTS

BUILDING RAPPORT
WITH STUDENTS

"Rapport" is an important word in the world of teaching. Teachers who have good rapport are usually more successful than teachers who don't.

But what *is* good rapport? It is more than just getting along well with students. It is also *respect*, a mutual respect between teachers and students.

How do teachers build rapport with students? The tips that follow give some practical advice.

Let students see you at after-school and evening activities, even if you don't have an assigned duty. It shows that you care about them and your school.

If you're not from the area where you teach, ask a native of your school district to give you a tour. Learning about the neighborhoods where they live will help you understand your students better.

Enjoy the students. If you enjoy them, they can tell, and they will enjoy you, too.

Never forget that students are the reason you are a teacher.

Remember what YOU were like when you were the age of your students.

View hall duty as an opportunity rather than a duty. It gives you a chance to build positive relationships with students outside the classroom. The efforts will enhance your rapport *in* the classroom.

Children are not miniature adults. Love them for what they *are*, not for what you want them to be.

Meet students at the door of your classroom. Smile and greet them by name. You will set a welcoming tone. The personal contact will also help build rapport.

Try to talk individually with as many students as you can each day. A few personal words will go a long way toward helping you earn respect and good will.

Listen to students.

Don't take yourself too seriously.

Understand that getting close to students gives them an important reason to succeed — to keep your personal opinion of them positive. Yes, it is better if they do well just to please themselves. However, at least in the beginning, your opinion may be all that some students have to lean on.

Remember that a student's hope is that he or she stands out, if not in the world, then at least in your eyes. Even when they're older and toughened and wise beyond their years, students still want to be noticed. They still want to feel important. Notice them.

Building Rapport with Students

Don't get too hung up on the way students dress. A student can have green hair and still learn algebra.

Building Rapport with Students

Try to pay attention to what movies, TV shows and music your students like. If you know something about their world, you know something about them.

In the
Classroom

IN THE CLASSROOM

A teacher's world is the classroom. So much takes place there — joy, disappointment, problems, growth, opportunity, advancement, laughter, tears, frustration, delight and so much more. No teacher experiences the same thing every day. There are highs and lows in teaching, just as there are highs and lows in life.

The tips that follow offer sound advice about the classroom, for teachers of all ages and any subject matter.

Recognize your power as a teacher. Use it for good.

Smile and laugh with your students. Enjoy them.

Learn your students' names as quickly as you can. (It's easier to say, "*Jason*, let me have that Walkman," than "Hey, you with the curly hair and the nose ring — let me have that Walkman.")

> Undeserved praise is a lie, and students know it. In trying to enhance self-esteem, don't get into the habit of praising what isn't really praiseworthy.

Tell your students, "Nobody wants you to succeed as much as I do." Make sure you believe it, and they will, too.

Students will learn more through **praise** than through criticism. Look for the good they do, and applaud them.

If you make it a top priority, learning names should take no more than two or three days, no matter how many students you have. (A seating chart helps a lot.) Your effort will let students know right away that you care about them and that you are serious about your job.

Don't give assignments you don't want to grade.

Rearrange the desks now and then. At the very least, change the seating arrangement from time to time. Sometimes a different seat in the room has an amazing effect on a student's attitude and/or behavior.

Keep reminding yourself, always: I am the adult here.

When passing out materials, stand in front of a row and count out the amount you need. Have students pass back the papers. Don't walk around and pass them out individually; it takes too much time and gives students an opportunity to misbehave. (This advice seems simple but it's surprising how many new teachers don't heed it.)

Students know busy work when they see it. Make sure everything you assign has a purpose, and make sure students know the purpose. (Note: they don't have to *agree* that the purpose is a good one. They just need to know what it is.)

When you say "no," mean it. Don't allow your students to talk you out of it.

Post plenty of instructional sayings around the room, and change them often. Some students are strictly visual learners. If nothing else sinks in all year, a good quotation might.

Set HIGH expectations. Your students will rise to your challenges.

Be honest and specific in giving positive feedback to students. Say, "Your second paragraph is really effective in creating a picture" — not "I really love your work." Say, "Your project is very creative and organized," not just "good job."

Don't try to ingratiate yourself by doing stand-up comedy in class. Be yourself.

Never ever miss the opportunity to embrace a "teachable moment."

Assume nothing.

Don't be surprised that you have to repeat instructions three or four times, or even nine or ten times. Also don't be surprised if, as a result, you sometimes feel like screaming or tearing your hair out. You're perfectly normal.

Smile.

Smile a lot.

Focus on the positive. Comment daily in each class about what you like. ("Thank you for waiting quietly." "Wow! You caught on to that right away!" "Nice job of improving your test scores this week.") A little praise goes a long way.

During quizzes, stay nearby. You can keep the frightened students from making the mistake of cheating. You can tap a dozing student on the shoulder with a pencil or pat a nervous student on the back. You are right there to say, "Good job!" or "You've only got three more lines."

Remember that students are the ones stuck in the desks. Move around a lot. Take a step or two toward students when you address them.

Provide a safe, structured environment in your classroom. For so many children, the world outside of school is scary and inconsistent, with few boundaries. Children crave consistency and structure. Establish a routine that they can count on, anticipate, even look forward to.

Make sure the class sees *you* learning, too.

If you have a hard time justifying a policy, procedure, action or assignment, even to yourself, take a harder look at it.

Tell students who you are. Don't give 40-minute talks about your dramatic and glowing past. But if the conversation happens to turn to pets, it's okay to tell them about your beloved but ugly dog Eggo. If the class is talking about horrible Christmas presents, go ahead and tell them about your spouse's habit of giving dismal stocking stuffers, like shoe laces and socks.

If you're feeling crabby, tell the students honestly, "I'm sorry if I'm a little edgy today. I couldn't sleep last night. I promise tomorrow to be warm, caring, gentle, happy, wise, brilliant and entertaining. But today — stay out of my hair." Most students respect this kind of honesty, though it won't work every time. Sometimes nothing works.

The last five minutes of class is a good time to let students unwind and gab a little. It is also a good time to *listen.* You can learn a lot if you open your ears to what students have to say.

Be kind.

Present material in many different ways, so that individual learning styles are addressed. A student who can't grasp anything if you TELL him about it may understand just fine if he gets to READ an explanation. Some students learn best if there is some sort of physical action involved in the lesson. Others excel when there is a lot of interaction with other people. Some work best working by themselves in a peaceful, quiet environment. Vary your lessons and activities as much as possible. Then you are more likely to reach everyone.

Invest in a camera. Take a lot of photographs in the classroom, and post them.

Use a color other than red to grade papers. Then you won't look like you bled all over the assignments. (But if you can't find anything except a red pen one night, go ahead and use it. You won't damage anyone's self esteem forever by using red now and then.)

> # Never lecture all period.
> # No one — no matter what age
> # — likes to listen that long.

Keep things in perspective. If a student writes profanity in a book, it's something to deal with. It's not time to reserve a cell in the penitentiary for the child. Similarly, if your lesson flops, don't berate yourself and look into becoming an accountant instead of a teacher. Learn from your mistakes. Laugh at yourself. Go on.

Never ever forget your sense of humor. If a student does something funny, laugh. If a situation is totally ridiculous, smile at its absurdity. Save up funny stories to tell your family and friends.

Don't plan a test on fire drill day.

Give students time to think after you have asked a question. Wait **a lot** longer than you think you should before you call on anyone. You will give more students a chance to participate, and you will encourage more thoughtful responses.

Students like to get off the topic. Sometimes that's fine. Sometimes it's not. Don't be afraid to get off the subject once in a while, especially if there is an opportunity for students to learn something important that isn't in the lesson plan.

Don't forget all the students in the middle.

The high-achievers get attention. The behavior problems get attention. The good students doing ordinary work are often ignored.

Be flexible. Don't fall apart when your lesson doesn't go exactly as planned.

If you are bored, the students are probably bored. Change something. Experiment with something different. Keep yourself interested, and the students are likely to stay interested, too.

Tell the truth.

Give in sometimes about little things.

Remember that every student is worth your effort. Some need affection and kindness most when they seem to deserve it least.

Spend more time on things you love. If you love teaching poetry, cut another unit a bit short and spend more time on poetry. Students will learn more about the subjects that *you* love.

Tell your students the first day of school that they do *not* have to ask permission to throw up.

Remember: Technology is a great tool, but not always appropriate. Chalk still works.

If "Read the chapter and answer the questions at the end" shows up in your lesson plans several times a week, you need to make some changes. The students probably aren't learning much.

You WILL have bad days. That's normal.

You WILL have great days. That's normal, too.

When students complain about teachers, yourself included, remind them that part of education is getting along with and learning from many types of people.

Share yourself with your students.

It will show them that it is okay to communicate and express emotions. If you are excited about becoming an aunt for the first time, tell them. If your grandmother is very ill, share your concern. Don't be aloof. Be a real person.

Always have a box of tissues on your desk, even if you have to buy it yourself.

Don't do something in the classroom unless you can see a reason for it. It may be fun to have fingernail painting contests or to watch funny movies, but what's the point? (There may be one. Just be sure you know what it is.) If you can think of no valid reason for an activity, don't do it.

Let students go to the bathroom, but never more than one at a time.

If you really want students to hear you, ask for "their eyeballs." If they are looking at you, they are much more likely to REALLY hear you.

Don't slam your hand on the overhead projector when you're angry. It is breakable.

Remember that the textbooks aren't always right — or even interesting. Don't treat them as gospel.

Ask yourself, every day, "What's really important here?" Is it more important to eliminate gum chewing, or to teach children to subtract? Is it more important to get students to use the correct heading on a paper, or to teach them to write clear, effective prose? Try to stay focused on what is really important.

Whenever you can, do an assignment yourself before you give it to your class. You will discover any problems with the lesson, and you will be able to help students more effectively with any difficulties they encounter.

Don't fret too much if you don't get through everything in the curriculum. Very few teachers do.

Expect the unexpected.

Don't criticize children for being immature. They are *supposed* to be immature. They are children.

Teach behavior and manners along with school subjects.

Don't fall into the trap of doing the same things exactly the same way every year. Re-experience your material. Try reorganizing or approaching a topic from a new direction. That way you *and* what you are teaching will remain fresh, lively and spontaneous.

Be positive.

Don't let grades become too important in your classroom. Remember that a good grade won't guarantee a happy marriage or a successful career. A bad grade doesn't mean a life of crime or a career saying, "Would you like fries with that, sir?"

If you want their attention, whisper.

Write with your students, and read with them. Share what you write and read.

In the Classroom

Don't teach your students to be pessimistic about the future. Let them learn that somewhere else. Make them feel in your class that they *can* change the world.

Have fun.

Always carry tissue, bandages, safety pins, cough drops and TLC.

Let students have input in their learning. Give them choices — always worded so that, no matter what they choose, they are choosing something you would want them to do anyway. (You don't have to let *them* know that.)

Set high but attainable standards for your students, and stick to them. Students usually perform to the level of their teachers' expectations. They (and, surprisingly, parents too) will try to whittle your standards down, but if you continually model high expectations, most students will work to meet them.

Don't be afraid to admit you don't know something. Tell students you will look up the things you don't know. Then do it.

Admit when you are wrong. You aren't perfect.

Always have pens or pencils for students to buy or borrow. Yes, they should bring their own, but sometimes it just isn't worth making an issue of it.

Every classroom has a great variety of student abilities. Some students struggle with reading and writing, for example, but shine at hands-on projects. Include a variety of assignments that will give all students a chance to excel.

Always be prepared. Students can "sense" a teacher who hasn't done her homework.

Act out of the conviction that your teaching matters. Believe that you will make a differ-ence. You will.

DEALING WITH DISCIPLINE

DEALING
WITH
DISCIPLINE

Many otherwise excellent teachers have failed in the classroom because they couldn't learn how to deal effectively with discipline. Discipline is a difficult part of teaching, and — like it or not — it is often what makes or breaks a teaching career. An out-of-control classroom is *not* a classroom where learning takes place, nor is it a healthy environment for students or the teacher.

But how does a person learn to have what is called "good discipline" in his or her classroom? A number of suggestions follow.

Listen to the old advice, "Don't smile until Christmas." It may be exaggerated, but the basic message is a good one. It's much easier to start out tough and loosen the reins later than it is to try and grab the reins after a class is running out of control. In other words, it is much easier to lighten up than to tighten up.

Be friendly toward your students, but don't try to be friends. Always remember that you are the adult.

Don't list 26 rules on the board and spend hours going over them. The students won't remember them. If a student has 6 classes, each with 26 rules, he or she has 156 rules to keep straight on any given day. That's just not realistic.

Decide what are the absolute basic, non-negotiable principles or rules for your classroom — no more than three or four of them. Carve these in stone (or write them in permanent marker). Then stick to them absolutely.

Don't threaten, unless you mean to follow through. If you threaten to keep the whole class after school, for example, the students won't believe you. You will just damage your credibility.

If you are having to deal firmly with an angry student, NEVER move toward the student. Instead, state your desire calmly but firmly and then turn AWAY, as though you expect the student to follow your instructions. That gives the student a chance to save face, and the confrontation is less likely to turn ugly.

Find an experienced teacher in your department whom students like and respect. Turn to that teacher when you need advice about discipline.

Enforce consequences consistently, but don't be ridiculously rigid. It's okay to make exceptions in unusual situations. You are in control.

Develop a system that lets you access things quickly. You don't have time during class to look for a file or staple a set of tests. While you are looking or stapling, students will find ways to keep themselves busy — and it probably *won't* be by getting right to work on their homework assignment.

Be fair.

Take your pick:

Involve students in the making of classroom rules. If they have a say in what they have to follow, they will be more willing to follow those rules.

OR

Don't involve students in the making of classroom rules, at least until you have several years of experience teaching. You are the teacher. You have to enforce the rules. You should be comfortable with them. (Students will often surprise you by making up rules that are far STRICTER than those you would choose. Then you are in the uncomfortable situation of enforcing those rules.)

Begin class immediately. Take roll later. Otherwise you will "lose" the students right off the bat.

If you feel yourself starting to dislike a student, take action immediately. If you allow dislike to take over, you can be sure the student will sense your feelings. The results will not be positive.

To help stop your negative feelings, find a way to talk to the student as one human being to another, about something *other* than class. Ask about the band pictured on a student's T-shirt. Ask his opinion about a new TV show on Monday nights. Ask about all the commotion in the hall last period. When you approach the student kindly, in a personal way, you are much more likely to find something to genuinely like in the person.

> Never embarrass or humiliate students, especially in front of their peers.

Be firm.

Seek cooperation rather than obedience.

Your job will be much easier if you win the respect of the "problem" students. Others will fall in line behind them. (However, be careful not to give them special treatment, or you will risk alienating the rest of the class.)

Never, ever get into arguments with students in front of the class. Tell angry or belligerent students that you will talk to them after class. If they persist in trying to start an argument, calmly repeat your request. Refuse to "take the bait."

Some students thrive on getting the teacher upset, just to entertain the class. Don't give them that satisfaction.

Don't raise your voice if a group is getting too noisy. Instead, speak more softly.

Trust your students until you have reason not to — but keep your eyes open. Be trusting but not naive.

Never tolerate disrespect from the students. *Expect* respect and *show* respect.

Be a leader, not a tyrant.

Always treat students politely and with respect. You may *feel* like swearing, smacking someone or ranting and raving. Do not.

Know when to play dumb. Sometimes it's better not to see a note being passed or not to hear a muttered comment.

Detention can be an excellent opportunity. Many teachers have won over some of their worst problem students by assigning them detention — and then visiting with them informally, one on one. Getting to know students and showing an interest in them often works wonders in changing classroom attitudes.

Learn a hard lesson right away: For some students, you are *rewarding* them when you reprimand them before the class. They have learned that negative attention is better than no attention at all.

Be aware that, no matter what age group you teach, your students are children. Even the oldest, the brawniest, the most mature, the most eloquent, the most confident is just a child. Do not, then, be surprised at anything your students do.

Discipline students in private, one on one. Give them time to calm down before assigning punishment.

Dealing with Discipline

If you are having trouble with a particularly difficult parent, a fringe group, an organization or anyone else connected with your school, start documenting all your conversations. Make a note of the conversation, the date, who was present and what was said. In the event of complaints, legal action, negative publicity or other action, your notes could prove very useful.

Tell your class that you, not the bell, will dismiss them. This may seem a small matter, but it will help you keep control of your class. It reminds students who is in charge.

Don't get really mad at your class more than five or six times a year. If an angry speech or stern lecture is extremely rare for you, the students will sit up and take notice. If they hear one every day, they will learn to tune you out.

Think of teens and preteens as caterpillars in cocoons, slowly breaking out of their shells, suddenly forced to deal with unfamiliar bodies and minds. Just as a newly released butterfly must adjust to its new body, which includes longer legs and huge wings, the developing teen must deal with big, clumsy hands and feet, changing body parts and unforgiving pimples. Try to imagine yourself in the same situation. Be kind.

Remember that *limits* help make a child feel safe.

Learn to recognize that "something is going on here that we don't want the teacher to see" look.

Be flexible, but not breakable.

Learn that you can agree to disagree. Not all disagreements can be resolved.

Do not rely on sending students to the office as a disciplinary technique. You will only become identified in the administrator's mind as "someone who can't handle his students." If you need help, try first to get advice from a teacher you respect.

Send only your most extreme cases to the office. Rely on the office as a last resort — probably no more than three or four times a year, total.

If a child does wrong, fault the behavior, not the child.

Be careful what you notice. If you don't have time right now to deal with students smoking, don't walk into a restroom with smoke pouring out the doors.

Remember that if students *see* that you see something, you have to act. Sometimes it's better not to see it.

If fights in the hallway scare you, don't be embarrassed. They scare a lot of people. Know your school's policy about what to do. Figure out a plan of action *before* you are faced with a fight.

Reward good behavior. It doesn't take much. Sometimes all it takes is just one jelly bean or a pat on the back.

Let students know that you are always willing to listen to complaints and suggestions, and that you will change a policy or a grade if the student presents a good argument. However, insist that students present their arguments in a mature, calm manner, either on paper or personally — and NOT while you are trying to teach class.

This guideline will help you separate students with serious complaints from chronic complainers or tantrum throwers. Students with legitimate concerns will talk to you after class. Students who just want to avoid responsibility for their actions usually won't bother. Neither will those who just enjoy entertaining the class by arguing with the teacher.

Trust your "gut." If something doesn't feel right, it probably isn't.

Never use sarcasm with a student. It doesn't work.

Make your classroom rules general to start out. You can always make them more specific later on.

Do what you say you will do. If you are scrupulous about it, you will have far fewer problems than teachers who do not.

The students are not the enemy. Never forget that.

COMMUNICATING
WITH
PARENTS

COMMUNICATING
WITH
PARENTS

If you develop a positive relationship with parents, students are the ones who will benefit most. However, *you* will also benefit by having allies in the difficult job of helping young people succeed.

Communicating effectively with parents is often simply a matter of common sense. Tell them what is going on in your classroom — and why. Treat them the way you would like to be treated as a parent. The ideas that follow can be helpful guidelines.

Remember that parents are not the enemy. Even the worst parents in the world usually want the best for their children, even if their actions may seem wrongheaded and counterproductive.

Remember that students usually get home before their parents. If you leave a

concerned message or send home a note, the parents may never see it. If you don't hear from them, try calling them at work, or at night.

If parents are blowing up at you, be quiet and listen. They are not going to hear anything until they calm down, so let them vent. (Phrases like "I understand what you're saying" help, too.)

Don't take parental attacks personally.

Okay, *try* not to take parental attacks personally.

Create an information form to use for parent conferences. Fill in student information before the conference, and go over a copy of it with the parent during the conference. This will help you organize your thoughts ahead of time, keep the conference focused and leave you with a written record of what was discussed.

Try to start and end parent/teacher conferences on a positive note.

Send postcards to parents to tell them all is going well or that you like having their child in class.

Set aside time regularly to make positive calls to parents, or to write positive notes. (A postcard takes two minutes to write. One per day adds up to 180 postcards per year.)

Tell how well a child is doing in your class, or that he got the highest grade on a test, or that you really appreciate the fact that she does her homework regularly — anything that can lead to a positive relationship with the parents. Many parents have never had someone call or write with *good* news about their child.

Only believe about half of what students say about home. Hope that parents do the same about school.

Involve parents as much as you can and keep them informed. When a student is not meeting the expectations in your classroom, academically and/or behaviorally, get in touch with the parents right away. Express your belief that you and the parent, working together, will help the child to be successful in the classroom. It is difficult for parents *not* to agree when you are talking about working together for their child's success.

Don't sit behind your desk at parent conferences.

Use your first name with parents.

Look parents in the eye and tell them "thank you" for their interest and attendance at a conference.

FITTING IN

FITTING IN

There's more to being a teacher than just going to your room and teaching. You also have to be part of a department, a school and a school district.

Your job will be easier and more enjoyable if the people you work with are friends and allies. It is possible to learn something from nearly every adult in a school system. Take a look at the following tips for fitting into your school environment.

Make a friend in your department or grade level. Glean ideas from them, raid their files, give them your undying loyalty and friendship — and maybe some lunches and milkshakes, too.

Never degrade other faculty or staff members in front of students. Call them by their proper names and speak respectfully of them, regardless of the situation.

Don't extend faculty meetings with too many questions that reveal your rookie status. Ask a trusted veteran later.

Keep a stack of note cards handy. Make time to dash off thank-you notes to deserving colleagues, administrators and students. They will appreciate them.

Ask the secretary to give you a tour of resources available in the office and school. There may be more materials available than you think.

Make friends with the school secretary. Secretaries have more power than you might suspect. Many of them practically run the school.

Don't offer your opinions the first year, unless asked. Listen and ask questions. Learn how your school works before you jump in with suggestions for reforming the educational system.

Be kind to the secretaries, custodians, cooks, bus drivers and other workers. They have a hard job, too.

TAKING CARE
OF
YOURSELF

TAKING CARE
OF
YOURSELF

Teaching is a hard job. It is hard to be "on" day after day after day, especially if you have a cold or didn't sleep last night or just feel generally out of sorts. It takes energy to motivate others and to deal with dozens of different personalities, learning styles, abilities, levels of accomplishment and family backgrounds.

You don't want to be a victim of teacher burnout before you have really begun. It is essential that you take steps to preserve your energy and enthusiasm for teaching. Try some or all of the ideas that follow.

Never make major writing assignments due the day before vacation. *You* need a vacation, too.

Take lots of vitamin C. Cold and flu season lasts from September through the middle of June.

Don't expect a social life until summer.

Don't try to be an interior decorator. Let students do the bulletin boards, unless it's something you really enjoy. You'll have more energy for other things.

You will spend a lot of time in your classroom. Make a comfortable spot for yourself. If you need a high stool to perch on as you talk to a group, get one. If a comfortable pillow in your chair will help, buy one. Invest in colored paper clips or bright file folders or a Far Side desk calendar — whatever will make your area feel comfortable and pleasant to you.

Take time out for yourself. Set aside

time regularly for something you enjoy — taking a dance class, knitting, playing on a soccer team, for example. A teacher **with** a life is better than a teacher **without** a life.

Invest in a good quality, roomy briefcase — one you love. You will be carrying it back and forth from home a lot.

> Feel glad that you are doing one of the most important jobs in the world. Your impact may not be felt for a while, but trust that you *are* having an impact on the future, through the young people you teach.

Learn how to operate and maintain all equipment — VCRs, the copy machine, the overhead projector, etc. Don't depend on others to operate them for you.

Don't feel guilty cutting into the front of the cafeteria line. The students don't have to go back to the classroom, eat, grade 30 tests before next period, check the mail in the office, call a parent, pick up an overhead projector from the library and fill out six forms for the principal — all in 25 minutes. You aren't a student anymore. You deserve certain privileges, just as you now have certain responsibilities.

Keep a journal. It will help you vent, let you brag to yourself about your accomplishments and become a place for you to record memorable incidents.

Invest in a simple tool box. It's sometimes easier and faster to fix a loose screw yourself than to wait for a custodian.

> When you have three dirty coffee cups on your desk, it's time to do some cleaning.

Don't sweat the small stuff.

Don't watch too many Hollywood movies about teacher success stories. They will only make you feel inadequate. Remember that the movies are only *loosely* based on real life. They don't show you all the ordinary days.

Wash your hands often, with soap and water. You will catch far fewer colds.

Take home only work you plan to do. Never take papers you think you *might* have time for. You won't.

Keep learning. Go to conferences, take classes, read. To be a great teacher, you must remain an avid learner.

Exercise, eat right and get enough sleep at night. Being fit is half the battle.

Keep a pair of latex gloves handy for medical emergencies in class or on the playground.

Learn CPR and other first aid techniques.

If you don't have a chance to go to the bathroom until fourth period every day, you might want to think twice about that second cup of coffee in the morning.

Do not take on too much in your enthusiasm. A tired or stressed out teacher is not the most effective teacher. Know your limits. Sometimes it's okay to say "no."

Make a "good stuff" file for yourself. There will be days when you wonder, "Why didn't I become a stock broker? I have absolutely no talent for teaching." On those days, dig out the file with the good stuff in it: the note that says, "You're my favorite teacher," or the evaluation from the principal that says, "Excellent lesson!" or the note that just says, "Thanks."

Designate at least one day of the weekend as a "No Schoolwork Day."

Keep an emergency folder with generic lesson plans for substitute teachers. If you come down with the flu, the last thing you want to do is drag yourself out of bed to write out detailed lesson plans.

Learn that a sense of humor is more valuable than the best lesson plan.

A Few
Words of
Wisdom

A FEW WORDS OF WISDOM

Teachers who have been around awhile have learned a few things about teaching over the years. It usually pays to listen to their advice.

There's an amazing amount of important "stuff" that is never mentioned in college classes. Some of this stuff can make or break a teacher's career. Learning to listen and to learn from your colleagues is a wise idea.

Consider the following words of wisdom from experienced teachers.

Find something to like in every student. There *is* something in every single one.

Behave in a way that elicits respect from others.

Don't whine, especially at school. No one likes a whiner.

If you teach in a small town, be aware that your behavior is public knowledge. If you snap at a waitress, people will know. If you get caught speeding, people will know. If you hang out at the bars a lot, people will know. Like it or not, your actions in your private life will affect your credibility and effectiveness in your professional life.

Ask for help when you need it. However, don't ask other people to do your job.

Think things through carefully before you buy a house in the neighborhood where you teach. You may not want to explain all your life choices to one of your fifth graders who lives across the street.

If you are close in age to your students, be especially careful not to become too familiar or casual with them. Maintain some distance and dignity.

Don't try to be liked by the students. The irony is, if you don't really care, they WILL like you.

Avoid situations where you are really alone with a student — for example, taking him or her home from school or working late together on sets for the school play. When you talk to a student one-on-one, be sure the door is always open and that others are always nearby. You will be less likely to leave yourself open to criticism or unwarranted charges.

Don't assume that being liked is the same as being respected.

Don't be drawn into (and definitely do not solicit) student gossip, especially concerning a fellow teacher or administrator.

Don't complain to the students about how little teachers make, or about how awful your job is.

Avoid discussing students with other teachers if there is any chance at all of being overheard. (Note: There is almost always a possibility of being overheard.) Be discreet.

Don't be afraid to share yourself with your students.
However, there's a difference between telling endless stories of your years as a high school football star and telling the students *one* story about an experience you had playing football.

Remember that you don't have to *like* all of your students in order to *care* about them.

Dress professionally. It will help students, parents and other teachers see you as a professional. It may even help you see *yourself* as a professional. (If you are very young, it will also help distinguish you from the students.)

When students complain about another teacher, don't take part in the criticism. Encourage them to discuss the problems with the teacher herself.

Never flirt with your students, even if they are almost the same age as you are.

If you feel afraid, pretend you are brave. If you feel crabby, pretend you are cheerful. If you feel unequal to a task, pretend that you can do anything. Often, pretending to feel a certain way will help you to actually *feel* that way.

Understand that students will remember little of what you teach, but much of what you model.

COTTONWOOD PRESS ORDER FORM

Please send me_____ copies of *Survival Tips for New Teachers*. I am enclosing $7.95 plus shipping and handling ($3.50 for one book, $2.00 for each additional book). Colorado residents add 24¢ sales tax per book. Total amount _____.

Name _____

(School) _____

Address _____

City _____ State_____ Zip Code_____

Method of Payment:

❑Payment enclosed   ❑Credit Card   ❑Purchase Order

Credit Card# _____ Expiration Date _____

Signature _____

Send to:

Cottonwood Press, Inc.
107 Cameron Drive
Fort Collins, CO 80525
1-800-864-4297

Call for a free catalog of practical materials for English and language arts teachers, grades 5-12.